W9-BAL-223

Eyeglasses

household history

Eyeglasses

Margaret J. Goldstein

Carolrhoda Books, Inc./Minneapolis

To Mom and Dad, who let me sponge off them

The author wishes to thank Dr. Jane West for technical assistance with this book.

Words that appear in **bold** in the text are listed in the glossary on page 46.

Carolrhoda Books, Inc., c/o The Lerner Publishing Group
241 First Avenue North, Minneapolis, MN 55401 U.S.A.

Library of Congress Cataloging-in-Publication Data

Goldstein, Margaret J.
  Eyeglasses / by Margaret J. Goldstein.
   p   cm. — (Household history)
  Includes index.
  Summary: Discusses the history and development of eyeglasses; includes a brief explanation of how the eye works and the vision problems that glasses can correct.
  ISBN 1-57505-001-3
  1. Eyeglasses—History—Juvenile literature. 2. Vision—Juvenile literature. 3.Vision disorders—Juvenile literature. [1. Eyeglasses—History.] I. Title. II. Series.
RE975.G65 1997
617.7'522—dc20   96-36450

Manufactured in the United States of America
1 2 3 4 5 6 – JR – 02 01 00 99 98 97

Contents

John Lennon didn't always wear his glasses.

"Oh! Say, Can You See?"

John Lennon, a member of the band the Beatles, had a great ear for music. His eyes weren't nearly so good, though. "He'd walk to the art college, past our school, with his glasses off," recalled a friend from John's teenage years. "I'd shout hello and he'd wave back to a lamppost or a postbox!"

John Lennon was typical of many young people. One out of every five children aged 6 to 16 needs glasses. About half of all grown-ups wear glasses. Most everyone needs glasses when they grow old. Why do so many people wear glasses? Why doesn't everyone see perfectly? The answer lies in light rays.

Light and Sight

Light is energy that travels through space. The sun gives off light rays. So do lightbulbs and candles. As light rays travel, they regularly bounce off objects and into your eyes. These light rays create images, or pictures, of the objects around you. Without light, you couldn't see.

Eyeglasses have been helping people see better for centuries.

Most people who wear glasses have healthy eyes. Their vision just needs a little fine tuning.

You couldn't see without eyes either. Did you know that your eyes contain tiny moving parts? A small opening called the **pupil** shrinks and expands to let different amounts of light into your eye. A clear disk called the **crystalline lens** grows thicker when you look at nearby objects and flattens for distance vision. All this moving and adjusting helps you see clearly.

For perfect vision, light rays must **focus,** or come together, at a single point on the **retina,** a layer of tissue at the back of your eye. The crystalline lens and the **cornea** (a clear covering in front of the eye) are responsible for *bending* light rays, sending them to the retina in the right direction. But the process doesn't always work perfectly.

Vision in a Normal Eye

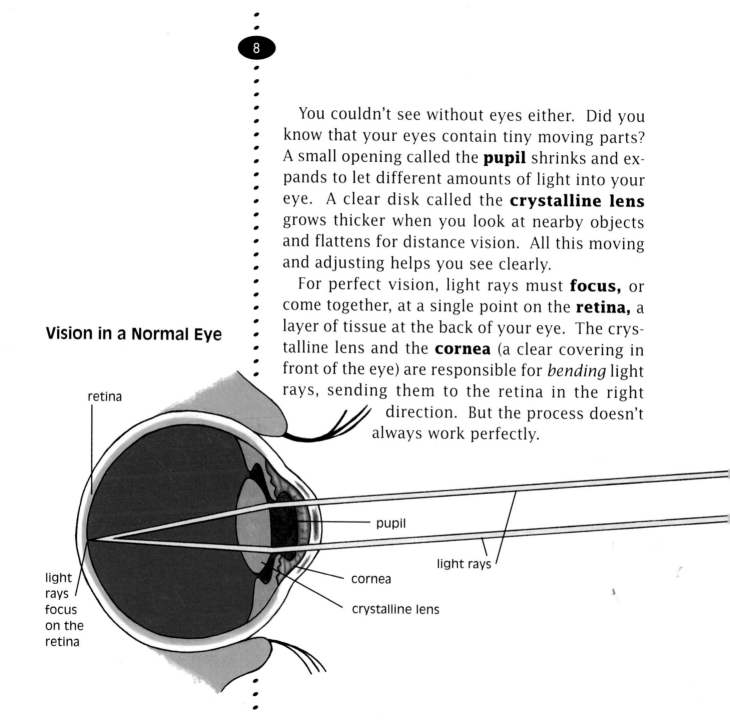

retina

pupil

light rays

cornea

crystalline lens

light rays focus on the retina

Nobody's Perfect

If your eyes are too long from front to back, or if your cornea is too curved, light rays will focus before they reach the retina. This problem is called **nearsightedness.** Nearsighted people can see nearby objects well. But faraway images, like street signs, are often nothing but a blur.

If your eyes are too short from front to back, or if your cornea is too flat, light rays will reach the retina before they focus. This problem is called **farsightedness.** To farsighted people, distant images look clear, but nearby images, such as words in a book, look fuzzy.

Another vision problem affects people after about age 45. As we grow older, our crystalline lenses stiffen. They can't thicken as easily as before. So reading and other close work become difficult. This problem is called **presbyopia** (prehz-bee-OH-pee-ah). The name comes from the Greek words *presbys* ("old man") and *ops* ("eye").

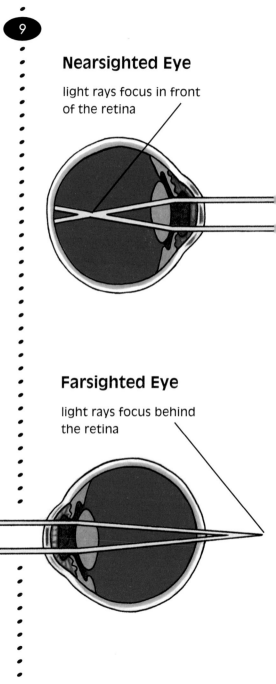

Nearsighted Eye

light rays focus in front of the retina

Farsighted Eye

light rays focus behind the retina

To see how light rays bend when they pass through lenses, put a spoon into a shallow glass of water. Look at the glass from the side. At the surface of the water, the spoon appears to bend. The water acts like a lens, bending light rays and changing the image you see.

A Precise Adjustment

Nearsightedness, farsightedness, and presbyopia are very common problems. Problems need solutions, and that's where eyeglasses come into the picture. Eyeglasses are available in many colors, shapes, and sizes. But no matter what the frames, or outside edges, of the glasses look like, all eyeglasses contain two clear disks called lenses. Sound familiar? Remember the crystalline lens?

Like the crystalline lenses inside your eyes, lenses in a pair of eyeglasses bend light rays. Unlike crystalline lenses, lenses in eyeglasses bend light rays *before* they reach your eyes instead of afterward.

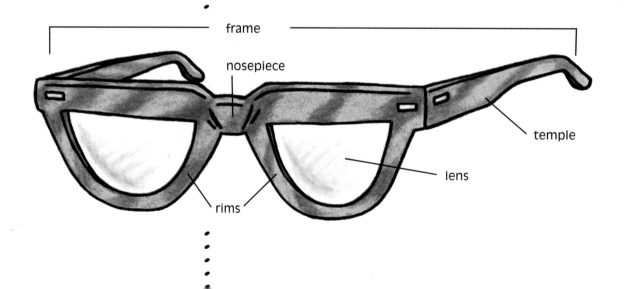

frame

nosepiece

temple

lens

rims

The shape of the lens is important because different kinds of lenses fix different kinds of problems. **Concave lenses** are thicker on the edges than in the middle. They correct nearsightedness. **Convex lenses** are thicker in the middle than at the edges. They correct farsightedness and presbyopia. In every case, lenses make a precise adjustment, bending light rays and sending them on to the retina at the proper angle.

With glasses, things look crystal clear.

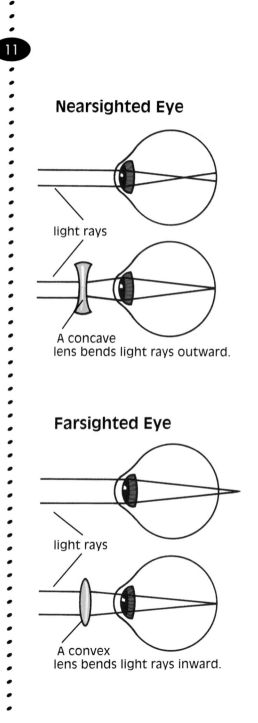

Nearsighted Eye

light rays

A concave lens bends light rays outward.

Farsighted Eye

light rays

A convex lens bends light rays inward.

What do microscopes, binoculars, and telescopes have in common? They all contain convex lenses. Convex lenses magnify, or enlarge, images. Another name for a convex lens is a magnifying glass.

You can make a magnifying glass. Fill a clear glass with water. Set the glass on a table, then hold a page from a book or newspaper behind the glass and look through the water. Do the words look bigger? You've made a convex lens—thicker in the middle than at the edges.

Just how far the light rays must bend to bring about clear vision depends on the person's eyes. Some people are more nearsighted than others. Some people are more farsighted than others. Eye doctors—**ophthalmologists** and **optometrists**—use special machines to examine people's eyes and to figure out exactly how much light-bending power each person's eyeglasses should have.

The person may have farsightedness *and* presbyopia. Or the person may have nearsightedness and presbyopia—and possibly even another vision problem on top of these. **Opticians,** people who make and sell eyeglasses, know how to make lenses that fix more than one vision problem at once.

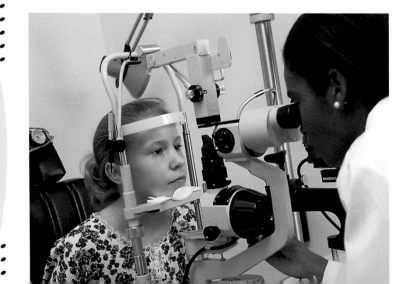

An optician can help you find frames that fit.

Seeing 20/20

Have you ever had your eyes examined? People with good eyesight are said to have **20/20 vision.** They can read all the letters on the doctor's eye chart from 20 feet away. If you can't read all the letters on the eye chart from 20 feet, or if you have trouble reading your schoolbooks, you might need eyeglasses. Your eye doctor can tell you what kind of glasses you need and can write a prescription, or instructions for the optician who will make your lenses.

If you need glasses, you're not alone. More than 140 million Americans wear eyeglasses—and people all over the world have been wearing them for hundreds of years.

Opposite page, bottom: A visit to the eye doctor

Hundreds of years ago, most people did not need perfect vision to do their work.

One of the Most Useful Arts on Earth

How did people see before eyeglasses were invented? Probably not very well. Of course, several thousand years ago, most people didn't need 20/20 vision. They were farmers, shepherds, and laborers. They didn't drive down busy freeways or read the daily newspaper. In fact, most people couldn't read and write at all.

In places such as ancient Greece and Rome, messengers announced the news out loud in city streets. Noblemen sometimes hired scholars to read books to them. But there weren't many books to read, anyway. Printing presses didn't exist. Scholars had to copy books by hand.

Even presbyopia, the failing eyesight of old age, didn't bother all that many people thousands of years ago. Medical knowledge was limited, and most people didn't live much past age 45.

Seneca, a first-century Roman leader and author, knew how to read, but he didn't have good eyesight. So he came up with a trick. He read books while looking through a glass jar filled with water. The jar of water acted like a magnifying lens, enlarging words on the page. Seneca didn't know that a lens made of clear crystal or glass, if cut to the right shape and thickness, would magnify images the same way.

Archaeologists have discovered convex lenses at the ruins of ancient Assyria, Arabia, Rome, India, and China. The earliest date from about 1200 B.C. These lenses were probably not used as magnifying glasses, but rather were "burning glasses." The lenses could focus the sun's rays onto a single point, creating enough heat to start a fire.

Long ago, scholars didn't have glasses to help them read and write.

Experiments and Observations

Over the centuries, people began to learn about **optics,** the scientific study of light. In about A.D. 1000, Alhazen, an Arabian scientist, observed how light rays bent when they passed through water and glass. He also studied the human eye. In his book on optics, Alhazen noted that objects looked bigger when viewed through a round crystal lens.

The English scientist Roger Bacon also studied optics. In 1268, he told about a "reading stone," a curved piece of crystal or glass that made written words look clearer and larger. The lens Bacon described simply rested on the page of a book.

Roger Bacon

Shortly afterward, historians believe, a craftsman put two such lenses inside two wooden frames, each with a small handle. He tacked the handles together and held the whole device before his eyes. He liked what he saw. Eyeglasses, or spectacles, as they were known back then, had been invented. Who was this inventor? No one knows for sure.

Who Was the First?

In 1289, an Italian writer gave some clues. "Without the glasses known as spectacles, I would no longer be able to read or write," he said. "These have recently been invented for the benefit of poor old people whose sight has become weak."

Another Italian, a monk from the city of Pisa, said in 1306, "It is not yet twenty years since the art of making spectacles, one of the most useful arts on earth, was discovered." The monk said he knew the man who made the first pair of spectacles. But he didn't mention the man's name.

In the 1350s, Tommaso da Modena made this painting, one of the first pictures of a person wearing eyeglasses.

These spectacles from the late 1300s are one of the oldest known pairs.

Another promising lead came from an Italian tombstone dated 1317. The stone reads: "Here lies Salvino d'Armato of the Armati of Florence, the inventor of spectacles. May God forgive his sins." For a while, historians credited d'Armato with the invention. Later, they discovered that the tombstone was likely a fake. D'Armato hadn't invented spectacles after all.

More clues about the first spectacles came from China. Marco Polo, an Italian explorer who traveled to Asia in the late 1200s, claimed to have seen aged Chinese people using lenses to help them read.

Marco Polo arriving in China

Most historians aren't convinced by Marco Polo's story. They think that spectacles to correct poor vision weren't used in China until the early 1300s, a few decades after they appeared in Europe. The true origin of eyeglasses remains a mystery.

Hooks and Handles

Early spectacle frames were usually made of wood, iron, or brass. But leather, animal horn, bone, and tortoiseshell were used too. In China, some frames were even made of papier-mâché. Early frames didn't have **temples** that rested on the wearer's ears. Instead, people held the spectacles before their eyes when they needed to read or take a close look. When not in use, spectacles could be slipped into a pocket or a fancy carrying case. Some frames folded in half, sort of like a pair of scissors.

Before temples were invented, people had to hold their spectacles.

Straps looped around the ears held this man's spectacles in place.

Soon people devised ways to wear spectacles without having to hold them. They rigged the frames with ribbons or leather straps, which tied around their ears or behind their heads. Some Chinese spectacle wearers tied strings to their glasses, attached small weights to the strings, and hung the weights behind their ears. So weighted down, the spectacles stayed put. Other people attached their spectacles to a hook or strap that tucked into a hat. "This method is only good for kings who take off their hats to no man," explained a character in an early book about eyeglasses, "but I am just a poor man who cannot use this method, for every time I doffed [took off] my hat the whole apparatus would fall to the ground."

Strings and weights kept spectacles on this Chinese man.

All the Better to See You With

In the early days, most lenses were made of clear gemstones, such as quartz or beryl, cut to the right shape and polished. The first lenses were convex, so they improved vision for people with presbyopia or farsightedness. In the 1500s, one writer told about a Spanish nobleman who liked to eat cherries with his spectacles on, so that the cherries looked bigger and juicier.

Not everyone liked the new invention. "It is much better and more useful that one leaves spectacles alone," wrote a German doctor in 1583. "For naturally a person sees and recognizes something better when he has nothing in front of his eyes than when he has something there."

The narrow slits running across these Inuit sun goggles allowed the wearer to see, but didn't let in too much sunlight.

People wore sunglasses long before they wore eyeglasses to correct bad vision. As early as 500 B.C., people in China protected their eyes from sunlight with the help of tinted crystals. Other early-model sunglasses blocked the sun's glare in snowy regions. The Inuit people of North America made sun goggles from thin pieces of wood, horn, or bone. Ancient Tibetans made sun visors out of finely woven horse or yak hair, and Siberian dogsled drivers shielded their eyes from sunlight with tin goggles pierced with small holes.

In spite of a few objections, eyeglasses caught on quickly, spreading throughout cities in Europe and China. Another device—the printing press—made eyeglasses all the more popular. Invented in Germany in the mid-1400s, the printing press helped people produce books, newspapers, and other documents quickly and in large quantities. Scholars no longer had to copy books by hand. More people learned to read, and more people bought eyeglasses to help them.

As books became more common, so did eyeglasses.

Early spectacles were used for seeing things close up.

Still, reading was not for everyone. Only the upper classes—kings, queens, and popes—learned to read in the 1400s and 1500s. A person who wore spectacles, therefore, was usually rich or important. So spectacles were something special. Paintings from this era show the wealthy and well known posing with spectacles in hand. One painting even shows Adam and Eve wearing glasses in the Garden of Eden! Eyeglasses had found their way onto the most famous faces. They had arrived to stay.

Perhaps this artist, Simon Bening, wanted to look important. He painted himself holding spectacles in the mid-1500s.

In the 1600s, more ordinary people began to wear glasses.

Spectacular Spectacles

As the years passed, eyeglasses got better looking and better to look through. Spectacle makers learned that eyeglasses with concave lenses could improve vision for nearsighted people. In the 1500s, Pope Leo X wore a pair to go hunting. He hit his targets like never before.

By the next century, lots of people were buying glasses, not just the rich and famous. In big cities throughout Europe, street peddlers and shopkeepers displayed trays filled with low-cost spectacles. There were no eye doctors then—no eye exams or prescriptions. Customers simply tried on pair after pair to find the eyeglasses that best improved their vision.

Elderly people tended to buy glasses with convex lenses—for reading and other close work. So these spectacles were called "old glasses." Younger people were more likely to buy eyeglasses with concave lenses—called "young glasses"—for distance vision.

Lenses were still made from gemstones, but glass was used too. Glass was cheaper and clearer than gemstones. At factories in Europe, craftspeople made lenses by cutting, grinding, and polishing small pieces of glass. Special lenses were made for spectacles and for newer optical devices: telescopes for looking at the stars and planets, microscopes for viewing tiny creatures in air and water.

This traveling salesman sold everything from eyeglasses to telescopes.

In Europe, eyeglasses became very popular.

*Eyeglasses worn by
American colonists in the
1700s*

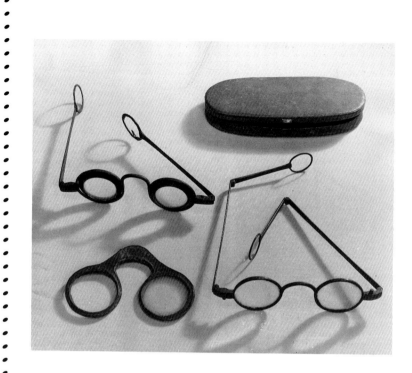

Benjamin Franklin

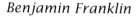

By the 1740s, European spectacle makers had added temples to eyeglasses. Hooks, straps, and weights were no longer needed. Glasses now rested comfortably on the ears and nose.

Across the ocean in North America, spectacles were harder to come by. Frames and optical glass had to be imported from Europe. This shortage didn't stop Benjamin Franklin—writer, scientist, and politician—from making an important contribution to eyewear technology in 1784.

concave lens

convex lens

A pair of bifocals from the 1960s.

Like many older people, Franklin (aged 78 at the time) needed lenses for both close and distance vision. Rather than switching back and forth between two pairs of glasses, he cut his lenses in half crosswise and made a pair of **bifocals**—with reading lenses mounted in the bottom half of the frame, distance lenses on top. Franklin's bifocals were not much different from the bifocals people still wear.

Seeing in Style

Ordinary people wore simple eyeglasses with metal frames and round or oval lenses—sometimes tinted for protection from the sun's glare. Lords and ladies preferred more elegant styles, made of ivory or gold and studded with jewels. The wealthy people of Spain liked king-sized glasses. "The greater a person's fortune," remarked a French countess visiting Spain, "the larger his spectacle glasses."

Aaron Burr (U.S. vice president in the 1800s) found a handy place for storing his spectacles—on top of his head.

The Chinese had their own eyewear traditions. The tortoise was sacred in China, and eyeglasses made from tortoiseshell were highly prized. Topaz, amethyst, and other colored crystals were considered lucky. Lenses made from these crystals not only shielded the eyes from bright sunlight, they also signaled good fortune for the wearer. Big frames were a badge of wisdom. Some Chinese noblemen wore big eyeglasses without lenses, just to show off, and common people were supposed to remove their eyeglasses when someone with a bigger pair entered the room.

Silver and crystal glasses (top), tortoiseshell frames (bottom). Both pairs are from China.

This Chinese spectacle case (right) was worn around the waist.

This pair of lorgnettes folds up into a case complete with a clock.

Lorgnettes (lorn-YETS)—popular in cities such as Paris, Vienna, and London in the late 1700s—were by far the fanciest eyeglasses of the era. Some were adorned with jewels or mother-of-pearl. The name lorgnette comes from the French word *lorgner,* which means to leer at, or stare. Lorgnettes were handheld eyeglasses. Instead of temples, they had an elegant handle, usually mounted off to one side. Sometimes the handle was placed between the lenses, which made the lorgnette look like a big, fancy pair of tongs.

Trendsetters held lorgnettes before their eyes at the theater or the opera for a better view. But for some people, being seen with an expensive pair of glasses was just as important as seeing the show. "Gentlemen and ladies [stared at] each other through spectacles," wrote Oliver Goldsmith, observing English theatergoers in 1762. With so many people using glasses, Goldsmith concluded that poor vision had become fashionable.

Lorgnettes were handheld spectacles.

A new eyewear trend swept Europe in the 1800s. The monocle was a single glass lens favored by professors, politicians, and anyone else who wanted to look important. Though some people thought a monocle was classy, it wasn't very practical. The wearer had to squeeze the muscles around the eye to keep the glass in place. Not surprisingly, monocles fell out a lot. But they were almost always equipped with a silk ribbon or gold chain, clipped to the wearer's jacket. So when monocles fell, at least they didn't fall to the ground and break.

Stylish people wore monocles in the 1800s and early 1900s.

Badly nearsighted, Theodore Roosevelt (at left in pince-nez glasses) got his first pair of glasses at age 14. "I had no idea how beautiful the world was until I got those spectacles," he said.

In 1912, while campaigning for a third term in office, Roosevelt was struck by an assassin's bullet. The bullet passed through a thick speech and a steel spectacle case in his coat pocket, before lodging in his chest. The spectacle case helped slow the bullet and most likely saved Roosevelt's life.

The next eyewear fashion appeared in the 1840s and lasted well into the 1900s. The style was called pince-nez (pahns-NAY), meaning "pinch the nose" in French. That is just how pince-nez stayed on, by means of a sturdy clip or tight spring between the lenses. Even so, the grip sometimes gave way. So pince-nez, like monocles, usually had a chain or ribbon attached.

By all reports, pince-nez weren't very comfortable. But they were extremely popular, pinching such famous noses as that of Theodore Roosevelt, 26th president of the United States.

Eyeglasses helped this shoemaker get the job done.

Now You See It

By the time of Roosevelt's presidency, in the early 1900s, the world had changed. Big cities had gotten bigger. New inventions abounded—airplanes, automobiles, movie cameras. Electric lights shone along city streets, in tall buildings, and inside people's homes. Aided by a clean, reliable source of light, more people learned to read.

Many young people left the family farm to attend college or to take jobs in the city. Whether they became bankers, secretaries, factory workers, or teachers, they needed good eyesight. And those who dared to get behind the wheel of an automobile had to be able to see where they were going!

The optical profession kept up with all these changes. By the 1900s, doctors understood the workings of the human eye. They knew how to fix nearsightedness, farsightedness, presbyopia, and more serious vision problems. The do-it-yourself method of fitting eyeglasses was over. Using new machines, eye doctors gave thorough vision exams to their patients and wrote prescriptions for lenses. Optical companies, such as Bausch and Lomb and the American Optical Company, produced frames and lenses.

In 1914 the American Optometric Association (founded in 1898) insisted that automobile drivers pass vision exams. When the United States entered World War I a few years later, thousands of men who failed their vision tests were rejected by the U.S. military. The message was clear: Americans who wanted to keep up had better look into some spectacles.

Above: Optician's advertisement, late 1800s

Since many early automobiles didn't have roofs or windshields, passengers wore goggles to protect their eyes from dust.

Here's Looking at You!

Zany 1930s film star Harold Lloyd was known for his horn-rimmed glasses.

During the early 1900s, pince-nez and monocles remained popular, especially among politicians and wealthy business tycoons. But average people needed glasses that weren't likely to fall off during a hard day's work. Most people wore simple steel frames, complete with temples that kept a firm hold on the ears.

Some people preferred thick round frames, made of tortoiseshell or animal horn. But both materials were costly and likely to break. Often, the so-called tortoiseshell and horn-rimmed glasses of the 1920s and 1930s were actually made of celluloid, a type of plastic. It could be molded and dyed to give a good imitation of the higher-priced materials.

The United States entered World War II in 1941, and this time men with poor vision weren't turned away by the armed forces. Instead, military doctors fitted a million servicemen each year with steel-framed eyeglasses. Aviators, anti-aircraft gunners, and sailors in tropical seas got government-issue sunglasses.

Above: Steel frames were common in the mid-1900s.

Left: Many World War II pilots wore Ray-Ban Aviator sunglasses.

Jazz musicians, such as Miles Davis, looked cool in shades.

Sunglasses have been used for centuries, but they weren't really popular until the 1930s. In that decade, movie stars such as Greta Garbo began to wear them—sometimes even indoors. Perhaps the stars thought they wouldn't be recognized in their dark glasses. Or maybe they just liked the glamorous, mysterious look the sunglasses gave them. Soon everybody wanted a pair.

In 1937 Bausch and Lomb, an American optical company, began selling Ray-Ban Aviator sunglasses. These were first designed to protect the eyes of Army Air Corps pilots. But with their handsome gold frames and smoky green lenses, Ray-Bans appealed to more than just aviators. General Douglas MacArthur wore a pair, as did thousands of other soldiers during World War II. The sunglasses stayed popular after the war.

A day at the beach in the 1940s

Dark lenses and sleek wraparound frames set the trend in the 1950s and early 1960s—especially among artists and musicians, who called their dark glasses "shades." Americans continued to copy their favorite stars. First Lady Jackie Kennedy launched a fashion trend in the 1960s with big, black sunglasses that became her trademark.

The latest trend has nothing to do with celebrities. Since the early 1980s, sales of sunglasses have skyrocketed in the United States. Scientists have learned that the ozone layer, the section of the earth's atmosphere that filters out ultraviolet rays from the sun, is growing thinner. Ultraviolet rays can harm our eyes. Fashion is still important to people who wear sunglasses. But more than ever, people are buying dark glasses to protect their eyes from sunlight.

First Lady Jackie Kennedy

Sunglasses help protect our eyes from ultraviolet rays.

After World War II, basic steel-framed eyeglasses fell out of style. Instead, many men bought sturdy square-rimmed glasses made mostly of plastic. Singer Buddy Holly, Clark Kent (occasionally known as Superman), and movie star James Dean all wore them.

Women's magazines featured ads for "cat's-eye" glasses, with plastic frames that flared upward at the temples. In 1953 Marilyn Monroe lit up the big screen in *How to Marry a Millionaire,* wearing rhinestone-studded cat's-eyes.

Buddy Holly helped make plastic frames popular.

Cat's-eye glasses had flair.

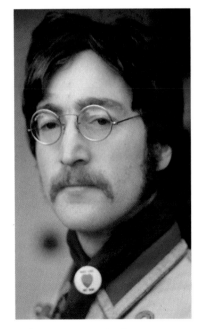

Plastic eyeglasses came in some funny styles, such as these "red devil" frames.

By the 1960s, plastic eyeglasses were big sellers. Plastic frames came in hundreds of shapes and colors. Some had zebra-skin stripes, others had leopard-skin spots. Few people wore metal-framed eyeglasses any longer.

Then along came John Lennon and the Beatles, the most popular musical group of 1960s. Most people didn't know that John was nearsighted. He rarely wore his black plastic glasses—especially not on stage. Then, in 1967, John switched to a pair of old-style steel-framed glasses with little round lenses. An old eyewear trend was new again. All of a sudden, young people wanted old-fashioned "granny glasses," just like John's. Antique stores did a brisk business in old metal frames, and eyewear companies rushed to make new frames in the old styles.

John Lennon in "granny glasses"

In the 1970s, glasses got bigger.

In the following decades, glasses wearers had all sorts of choices. Some people bought granny glasses. Others preferred big plastic frames in bright colors. Some people wore "half-moon" reading glasses, which rested on the end of the nose. Other people liked aviator-style glasses.

By the 1990s, horn-rimmed and tortoiseshell styles had made a comeback. So had cat's-eyes. The "classics" had returned, though brand-new styles were always being added. Plastic lenses had largely replaced glass ones. Plastic is lighter than glass and won't easily break.

Eyeglasses come in all shapes and sizes.

Even with many styles to choose from, a lot of people don't want to wear glasses—at least not all day long. Eyeglasses might slip down your nose on a hot day or fall off during a rough game of basketball. Many people wear **contact lenses** as an alternative. Contact lenses are tiny, clear pieces of plastic that float on a layer of tears, right on the cornea of the eye. They bend light rays and correct poor vision, just as eyeglasses do. But they're almost invisible, and they won't fall off during sports and games. Because contact lenses need special care, doctors suggest that young people wait until their teens before trying them.

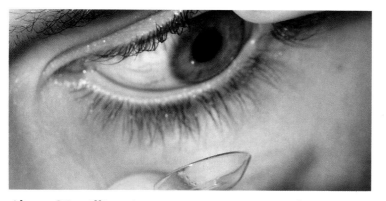

About 25 million Americans wear contact lenses.

Eyeglasses can be serious or silly. One silly pair has battery-powered windshield wipers—great for rainy days. "Nose glasses," available at toy stores, are good for costume parties. They have bushy eyebrows and a big plastic nose attached. "Eyeball glasses," with fake eyeballs that bounce around on springs, give new meaning to the term "pop-eyed." Silly eyeglasses won't improve your vision, but they're fun to wear.

That Smarts!

Some people think that glasses are just for smart kids. After all, think of all the brainy glasses wearers in stories and cartoons. There's Simon the smart chipmunk on *The Alvin Show,* Sherman and Mr. Peabody on *The Bullwinkle Show,* and Marcie from the *Peanuts* comic strip. Not only do all these characters wear glasses, but they also tend to be smarter than everyone else in the story.

Will glasses make you smarter? The answer is no. The connection between eyeglasses and brain power is a myth—going back to the earliest days of spectacles. Glasses won't make you smarter, and being smart doesn't mean you need glasses. If you can't see well, however, you might not do your best at school. So if you have a vision problem, glasses might help you improve your grades.

Sherman and Mr. Peabody

Marcie often gives advice to her Peanuts *friends.*

Who wears glasses and contact lenses? Thirty percent of the U.S. Olympic team in 1996, for starters. Filmmakers Spike Lee and Steven Spielberg wear glasses. Actress Darryl Hannah loves glasses. She owns more than 60 pairs! In a funny book called *Glasses: Who Needs 'Em?* by Lane Smith, a young boy learns that, in fact, he needs glasses. He isn't happy about the news. But when he hears about the interesting characters who wear eyeglasses, they start to look better to the boy—especially after he puts on a pair.

Eyeglasses are for seeing. They're also for being seen. Visit an optical shop, try on a few pairs, and look at yourself in the mirror. You might not believe your eyes.

Darryl Hannah wore cat's-eye frames in the movie Steel Magnolias.

Moviemaker Spike Lee

Crafty Eyeglasses

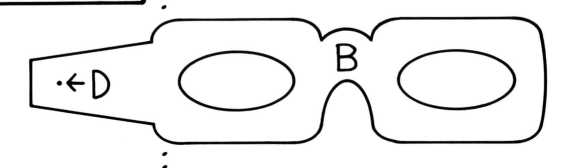

Make a pair of fold-up lorgnettes, eyeglasses used by people in the 1700s who wanted to see and be seen.

You Will Need:

tracing paper

pencil

poster board

scissors

a thumbtack

one brass paper fastener

tape

glue

decorating supplies: colored pencils, markers, paints, sequins, glitter, ribbon

• ← C

A

1. Use the tracing paper and pencil to trace patterns A and B. Mark dot C and dot D as you trace. Cut out the patterns, including the insides of pattern B.

2. Place both of the patterns on poster board and trace around them. Trace piece A twice. Cut on the lines. Have an adult help you cut out the insides of piece B.

• ← D

B

3. Place your tracing patterns over pieces A and B again. Use a thumbtack to carefully make holes at dot C and at dot D. Remove the patterns, then use a sharp pencil to make the holes a bit bigger. Place piece B between the two A pieces and insert the paper fastener through all three holes. Spread the ends of the fastener. Tape pieces A together at the end opposite the paper fastener.

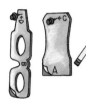 

4. Fold piece B at the center of the nosepiece. Tuck the eyeglasses into the handle, and you have a pair of fold-up lorgnettes.

5. Decorate your lorgnettes with paint, sequins, glitter, ribbon, or anything else you can think of. Now look at someone through your splendid spectacles!

Pipe Cleaner Specs

To design your own pair of eyeglasses, all you need are some pipe cleaners and a pair of scissors. First, shape two rims out of pipe cleaners—make them round, square, or whatever shape you like. Then make a nosepiece by attaching the rims with a short piece of pipe cleaner. (Now you have a pince-nez!) Next add temples; attach a pipe cleaner to the outside of each rim and bend the ends to fit around your ears. Try the glasses on. Maybe you'll start the next eyewear fashion.

Glossary

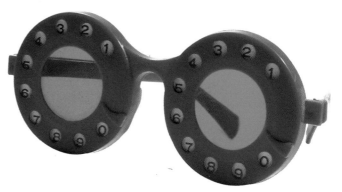

bifocals: eyeglasses with lenses for both distance and near vision combined in one frame

concave lenses: pieces of glass, or another clear material, that are thicker at the edges than in the middle. Concave lenses correct nearsightedness.

contact lenses: small, clear pieces of plastic that fit over the cornea and correct common vision problems

convex lenses: pieces of glass, or another clear material, that are thicker in the middle than at the edges. Convex lenses correct farsightedness and presbyopia.

cornea: a transparent tissue in the front of the eye. The cornea bends light rays as they enter the eye.

crystalline lens: a clear, flexible structure inside the eye that bends light rays

farsightedness: a vision problem created when light rays reach the retina of the eye before focusing. Far-sighted people see distant objects clearly but have poor near vision.

focus: to meet at a common point, as when light rays meet inside the eye to create an image. An image that looks clear and sharp is said to be "in focus."

lens: a curved, transparent disk, such as a piece of glass, that bends light rays

nearsightedness: a vision problem created when light rays focus before they reach the retina of the eye. Near-sighted people see nearby objects clearly but have poor distance vision.

ophthalmologist: a medical doctor who specializes in treating the eye and its diseases

optician: a person who makes or sells eyeglasses and contact lenses

optics: the scientific study of light—how it travels, changes, and produces images

optometrist: a doctor who specializes in visual problems that can be corrected by eyeglasses

presbyopia: a vision problem created by the stiffening of the crystalline lens. People with presbyopia have poor near vision.

pupil: a round opening in the eye that expands and shrinks to let in different amounts of light

retina: a layer of tissue at the back of the eyeball that turns light rays into visual images

temples: the supporting pieces of a pair of eyeglasses that rest on the wearer's ears

20/20 vision: good eyesight, defined by a test of a person's ability to read a chart from 20 feet away

Three-dimensional, or 3-D, glasses have special lenses that can make a comic book or movie look more realistic.

Index